Boom Town Reflections

Volume - 2

The Odyssey Begins

Mark A. Gregg

This book is dedicated to Vangie, the most amazing woman in the world. She is my wife, soulmate, and best friend. We have lived every moment of this incredible journey together. No one knows her fierce tenacity and genuine tenderness like I do.

Table of Contents

~1~
THE PHONE CALL

His eyes... The incredible depth of wisdom and total sincerity of his eyes. This memory haunted me. After only meeting a scant hour earlier, the CEO of Wurlitzer organ company made a simple promise that he and his wife would pray for me to get my wished-for job in a power plant. It was a surreal moment that was etched into my memory forever.

Each time my thoughts drifted back to that moment I still wondered, —*Who even does this?*‖ He was obviously educated and wealthy and yet in an act of gratitude he authoritatively and with an air of certainty told me the God of the universe heard his prayers and would answer. *I really wanted to believe him now more than ever.* Unfortunately, life had taken some negative turns in the months since this proclamation.

After Vangie and I's marriage between our Junior and Senior year in high school in 1974, I continued being a car mechanic in Montrose, Colorado. While I never had any formal training, I was improving steadily due to my upbringing and involvement with racing.

Through a chance meeting I rebuilt a 1970 Dodge Challenger powered by a high performance 426 Hemi for an older insurance salesman named John Willard. He may have been physically more than twice my age, but mentally and emotionally was still an out-of-control teenager. *Unfortunately,* we hit it off and became friends. John decided I would make an amazing Medicare supplement insurance salesman. His superb and tightly honed sales ability was advanced enough that I believed him. *He* was the consummate salesman, certainly not me. *It was an unmitigated disaster.*

This fleeting and miserable period was one of the most flawed decisions I ever made. I quit being a mechanic and became a door to door Medicare supplement insurance salesman. I sold two policies in three months. It was the worst, most depressing, debilitating job I have ever had to this day.

In the evenings I would return home completely exhausted, mentally and emotionally, from knocking on doors of social security recipients. I would tell Vangie that even though I was unable to sell anything, I, at the least, made some good friends. Most of the elderly people I visited were lonely and just dying to talk to *anyone*. Heck, *many were just dying.*

The crazy thing is, I enjoyed listening to all these people and their unique stories... Right up until I began to get seriously depressed. We were living off meager _advances' that John gave me as I was —learning the business.‖ These advances were barely paying the bills.

I abhorred the continuous rejection and failure, and quickly realized I could never do this or anything close to it as a career. I then pretended not to be depressed and would knuckle down, working even harder to sell this crappy, Medicare-supplement insurance. Nope! This Wasn't *ever* going to happen.

After I couldn't take the rejection any longer, I was lucky enough to find a job with Corelli Motor Company. It was a used car lot opening on the north end of Montrose, Colorado. The mercurial owner, Emmet Corelli, just finished building a large new shop that included an excellent complement of equipment and tools. It was a nice facility.

Emmett had lost an arm in WWII and picked up the moniker, _one-armed bandit' in Montrose. He wasn't a bad guy. Initially, he was a decent boss and had always been an excellent car salesman. I'm certain he could sell salted peanuts at a 200% mark-up to someone dying of thirst.

The mechanic's job at Corelli's demanded extensive hours. I was the only person in the shop, and Emmett tended to buy and take a lot of troubled vehicles, mainly four-wheel- drive pickups, as trade-ins.

Luckily, the job included medical insurance because a few weeks after accepting it, Vangie found out she was pregnant with our first child. I was both excited *and* pensive. Graduating from a carefree, hard-drinking teenager to a responsible, teenage dad was *almost* sobering.

With Vangie and I working full time, money was now less of a problem. We wanted to buy a house, and our first opportunity arose through a low-income, home-purchase program. It was for first-time home buyers whose income fell into our range. We fit all the criteria necessary and became _bonafide' property owners.

The low-income homes were outside Montrose on a winding, eight-mile-long gravel road known as Marine Drive. The homes were brand new, each on an acre of undeveloped land. Every home had an identical floorplan, providing 1200 square feet of living space with three bedrooms.

We could barely believe it, but we purchased our first home on an acre of land for approximately $27,000.00 in a beautiful area of Colorado. We were both elated that our new baby would be brought into the world in a brand-new home with a big yard.

This was the last good news we had for a while. In the final few months of Vangie's pregnancy, the job at Corelli Auto Sales began heading south. While I hate excuses, I was 19 years old and tasked with every conceivable repair imaginable with no formal training and limited experience.

I was expected to deftly rebuild 4WD transfer cases, differentials, and transmissions (automatic and manual), and take on other repairs of every imaginable sort. Even in large car dealerships, the mechanics had specialties. Not me. Working for Emmett, I was expected to know *everything* about *everything.* It is no wonder I was failing.

Corelli sold more four-wheel drive trucks than anything else, most of which were to farmers and ranchers...People he considered his friends. These trucks were abused and poorly maintained and I was expected to repair them quickly and inexpensively.

My claim to fame? Stupidity. Seriously. I would plunge headlong into a project where angels feared to tread. It had always been this way. The difference now was Emmett tracked the costs of these repairs and was seeing too many of them going wrong. *Way wrong.*

My mental state was deteriorating because we were in a new home, and I could see that my poor work performance was costing me my job. How did I pay for the new house? What about the car payment? What about the multitude of other bills? I did the reasonable, intelligent, logical thing that anyone would do under these circumstances; I began drinking heavier than usual.

Even if the job wasn't going well, Vangie's pregnancy was. She was a small-framed girl carrying what appeared to be a huge baby. She glowed. Even now, she is the most beautiful woman I have ever known, but when she was pregnant, it was amazing how pretty she was.

The weeks to delivery dwindled to days. We were about to enter a new, complex phase of life called parenthood. Thursday, October 28th, 1976, Doctor Richard Gingery hospitalized Vangie, inducing labor. She was due, and he was leaving town on vacation. Vangie did not want someone else to handle the delivery. I proudly suited-up and was present for the entire delivery.

During the delivery, I sat at her head, held her hands, and acted as her coach right up until I fully hyper-ventilated. This was two, or three minutes into the eight-hour delivery process.

Per the Doctor's orders, I had to sit in a chair with my head between my legs. However, watching Vangie give birth to our new little girl was an amazing, life-changing experience. I realized just how tough and strong my wife was/is. Not a peep throughout the entire birthing process. She was a trooper from beginning to end.

We named our beautiful new daughter Brandi. She weighed 7 Lbs., 3 ounces, and was, in a single word, PERFECT. They released Vangie and Brandi from the hospital the following day.

At our new home on Marine Drive, I diligently cared for both Mama and Daughter. Even though she was completely silent and strong during the birth, she was hurting quite badly the next couple of days.

Vangie had decided to bottle feed Brandi, so I could do the formula and bottle, feeding her and taking care of her. I felt like it was one of the few things I did well when I was 19 years old. I absolutely cherished that little girl.

Have you ever smelled the breath of a newborn baby? It is an enveloping, euphoric experience. Studying her tiny little fingers and toes filled me with wonder and fear.

What if something happened to her? I could not even think about it without crying. I was so in love with this tiny little cherub, part me and part Vangie, that the smallest thought of something happening to her would break my heart and immediately induce tears.

I took a week of vacation after Brandi's birth to stay home and help Vangie. I needed the vacation due to the pressure I was under at work from my waning job performance.

That fateful morning, Monday, November 1st, 1976 I was in the front room feeding Brandi from a bottle when the phone rang. It was **THE CALL** I had been praying and longing for! A Shift Supervisor named Joe Johnson, called from the Jim Bridger Power Plant in Rock Springs, Wyoming. He wanted me to come for an interview to be an Operations Helper at the plant. This was a fancy term for a *laborer.*

I couldn't believe it! My first thought was William Hurlemann's proclamation that he would pray for me to get a job at a power plant. I somewhat dismissed it, but it was always on my mind.

Joe emphasized that the helper position only paid $4.25 an hour, but the potential for advancement was genuine because this was a huge, coal-fired power plant that was still growing. He asked if I would be willing to come to Rock Springs at my own expense for an interview. Are you serious? This is a dream come true. I would have *WALKED BAREFOOT* to Wyoming for the interview!

After getting off the phone with Joe Johnson, I ran into the bedroom and told Vangie about the call and the request for an interview. I was incredibly excited.

Though tired, she responded to my pronouncement with a smile and a, —Good! I think that's great.‖

Vangie rarely responded to anything with visible outbursts of emotion. This was no exception. She was very much like her dad,

Alex. He remained low-key and didn't say much, but when he did, you had better listen. There is a Latin proverb that states *"Still waters run deep."* I think this best describes Vangie and her dad. Beneath the quiet exterior, there is a strong, rugged intellect and a matching passion that didn't rise to the surface often but was quite formidable when it did.

~2~
A GLIMMER OF HOPE

In 1977 the venerable CBS news program —60 Minutes exposed life in the —Old West Boom Town of Rock Springs, Wyoming. It was replete with murder, drugs, prostitution, corruption, and every conceivable type of human suffering. It was also a very accurate look at an area experiencing life in a way that most people thought ended at the turn of the 19th century 76 years earlier.

It was quite a shock for a naïve, 19-year-old, small-town Colorado family to go to Rock Springs, Wyoming, in 1976 with a young bride and baby. In fact, I would say it was a defining moment in our lives.

A boomtown is typically defined as a place experiencing rapid growth in both business and population, but this definition hardly captures the staggering and almost overnight surge of activity in Sweetwater County, Wyoming, during the mid-1970s. In my view, a boomtown consists of two kinds of people: those desperately seeking a chance for a better life, and those who profit from their desperation.

Located just 15 miles from Rock Springs, Green River, Wyoming, was also swept up in the boom, largely due to its vast deposits of trona, the largest known in the world. Trona, or trisodium hydrogen decarbonate dihydrate, is a non-marine evaporite mineral mined from massive underground deposits. It's the primary source of sodium carbonate in the U.S., an essential component in products ranging from glass and chemicals to household detergents and baking soda. Visiting a trona mine feels like stepping into a colossal box of baking soda or an immense, frozen cavern without the freezing temperatures.

In the 1970s, the trona mines in Green River were rapidly expanding, requiring them to construct an enormous supporting infrastructure, including power plants, processing, and packaging plants. Because Green River is only 15 miles from Rock Springs, the influx of workers to fill badly needed construction and technical jobs completely overwhelmed Rock Springs and Green River. Anytime you have an economic boom of this magnitude, opportunists, crooks, savages, politicians, and similar vermin with self-serving agendas slither in like a cockroach infestation in a filthy tenement.

Besides the trona mines in Green River, Rock Springs was also very near several large coal mines and the brand- new Jim Bridger coal-fired power plant. This plant, at completion, consisted of four separate generating units, each producing 500 megawatts. This is 2,000,000,000 total watts of electrical power being generated by an energy source whose abundance fueled the industrial expansion of the United States.

In 1976, Coal provided most of this nation's dependable, abundant electrical energy. To put this into perspective, over 2.6 million horsepower is generated by the four steam turbines at the Bridger Plant. Is there any wonder why a gearhead like me wanted to work in a power plant?

In 1976, laborers were in extreme demand at most of the huge industrial plants, coal mines, and trona mines. The problem at the Jim Bridger power plant was the union contract. The contract stated that entry-level personnel must start employment on the ladder's bottom rung. You were either a maintenance helper or an operations helper. It was nothing more than an entry-level laborer's position. It paid $4.25 an hour. Few people wanted this job as it was not even close to a living wage in Sweetwater County in 1976. It forced people like Joe Johnson to hire people like me from other areas, usually far away from Rock Springs. Granted, I sent them a lame resume because I wanted to work in a power plant more than anything else in life. ***I just didn't realize a coveted power plant position in Rock Springs was bundled in several layers of hell.***

During my initial phone call with Joe Johnson, he explained that I must take some written tests requiring knowledge of basic math, algebra, and mechanical fundamentals. He said passing the test was essential for being hired. I had Algebra – 1 at Montrose High School in Montrose, Colorado. I did well, passing with my customary D or D-. *What? Did you expect higher?*

Due to my lack of educational prowess, I was incredibly nervous about the upcoming algebra test promised by Joe Johnson. So much so that I went to the Montrose Public Library and checked out several books on basic algebra. After jumping into them, I realized that I probably should have paid a bit more attention at Montrose High. It was apparent I missed a few things like, maybe, *addition*, *subtraction*, and *basic mathematics*. Because of this, I knuckled down and studied the algebra books. The more I got into it, the more my anxiety level increased at the upcoming exam.

My interview was scheduled three weeks after that fateful call to come and interview. Work at Corelli Auto Sales was quickly going downhill, and I was trying my best to help Vangie with Brandi while intensely trying to consume the algebra books. The thought of not passing the tests and missing out on the job at Bridger panicked me.

My latest spectacular acts of gross incompetence at the car lot had them watching me like a hawk. They were not allowing the smallest discrepancies to go unnoticed. Though not very bright, I was smart enough to see my time at Corelli's was coming to an end.

I was pleased that Vangie accompanied me to the interview in Rock Springs. She wanted to see her potential future home. We could do this because Alex and Cordie graciously volunteered to watch Brandi.

Because we were essentially broke, the trip was to be a quick one. The blackness of night had fallen when we finally passed the Bridger Plant several miles to the north of I – 80 on our way to Rock Springs. Even though the plant was several miles away, it was a bright and impressive sight with the veil of darkness as a backdrop. Seeing it loom large in the distance added to my excitement and anxiety about the test.

We checked into a flea-bag motel near the eastern exit of Rock Springs. It was clearly void of any recent exterior maintenance, and the rooms were, not surprisingly, in equally poor shape. At that young age, I equated crappy to cheap, and we certainly required cheap.

We moved beyond the revulsion of the grimy and outdated room by voraciously indulging in a large plate of Chinese cuisine at the Sands Café, a few blocks away from the motel.

Rock Springs was rife with Chinese restaurants. Many were descendants of laborers that were pressed into service at the mines and with the railroads in a past generation.

With full stomachs and guarded excitement, we explored Rock Springs without a clue where we were going. It was clearly an old coal mining town with an emphasis on *OLD*. We stumbled into the downtown area, and it was not a nice, clean slice of Americana like Montrose. No, it was decidedly rundown, dreary, and foreboding. There were noisy, bustling bars galore, and the streets outside the bars featured their own vibrant but salacious economy.

If it was illegal, it was available in downtown Rock Springs. Vangie was even more reserved than usual. Looking back on it, I realize it was her stoic desperation at the prospect of raising our new daughter in this blight. Whatever she was thinking, she internalized it and said nothing, a common trait of hers.

We decided to travel back to Montrose by driving Highway 191 from Rock Springs to Vernal, Utah. We chose to go through Baggs Wyoming coming to Rock Springs because Highway 191 required passage through the rugged Uinta Mountains in Utah. The top of Flaming Gorge Pass is over 10,000 feet and could be quite treacherous in the winter. However, after driving the tedious and mind-numbing trip through Baggs and I-80, the snowy mountains seemed like a welcome relief.

Vangie stayed at the motel the next day since I needed to pass through Rock Springs again to take Highway 191 into Utah. This way, I could easily pick her up before we continued on toward Montrose. I left for my interview early that morning, making sure I had plenty of time to avoid being late.

~3~
THE INTERVIEW

I was excited, anxious, and dealing with heart palpitations due to the adrenaline surge as I viewed the plant in daylight for the first time. It was larger than life! Three generating units (three separate generating stations) already operating, and the fourth unit was under construction. The four towering smokestacks thrust majestically into the dark blue sky. I was in awe at the billowing white vapor clouds ascending aggressively into the heavens from the cooling towers.

I parked the car and pensively entered the administration building, admiring the expensive furniture and brickwork. There was a large reception area in the middle of the admin building surrounded by window-lined offices. The constant din of the plant was ever-present in the background but amplified many times as people opened and closed the office doors passing back and forth from the plant. I was the first to arrive of five other young men who came to interview for the Helper's job.

After giving my name to the receptionist, I sat for an eternity waiting to meet Joe Johnson. During the wait, I stealthily observed the attire and grooming of the other applicants as they skulked in. I must have looked like a Sunday school teacher to them. They were sloppily groomed and poorly dressed, and the one sitting next to me clearly wreaked of alcohol. After sitting sloppily in his chair for a few minutes, his chin dropped to his chest as he fell asleep, noticeably snoring.

I was shocked that a job this impressive did not bring out the absolute best in everyone who applied. I had yet to grasp that the

$4.25 an-hour starting wage made it almost impossible for the plant personnel to get decent people in that inflated boom area.

Joe finally arrived on the scene wearing a lightweight plaid shirt, blue jeans, and work boots. He appeared to be a trouble-free, laid-back guy, but I would later learn he was not near as laid back as he appeared that day. He was a tall, lean redhead in what I would guess was his middle 30's. He appeared to chain-smoke cigarettes and spoke with a noticeable Southern drawl.

As each applicant shook his hand, he sized us up with his eyes. I made darn sure I squeezed his hand as hard as I could. He had a very firm handshake as well, which made me feel good about him.

Joe gave a quick speech about the excellent possibility of advancement in a new plant like Bridger, but we had to pass the entrance exam to be interviewed for the job. He then ushered us into a common area on the other side of the reception area and handed out the tests.

Looking sternly at us he carefully announced, —Please do not turn the tests over until I give the word.‖ He subtly pointed to his watch and finished with, —These are timed tests.‖

A timed test? *REALLY*??? He never said anything about this on the phone. I was now officially freaking out. It is bad enough to give a 19-year-old high school drop-out a test, but to limit the amount of time available to *guess* the answers was just plain mean!

He continued rhetorically providing instructions by saying, —Don't waste your time on any single question. Just move on to the next question if you don't immediately know the answer.‖

I was the first and only person to demurely raise my hand.

He stopped his discourse when he saw my hand go up. —Yes, Mr. Gregg, you have a question?‖

—How many tests are there?‖ I asked timidly, already worried sick about the potential outcome.

—Good Question!‖ He exclaimed. —There are five tests. They are Reading Comprehension, Mechanical Concepts, Mathematical, Spatial Reasoning, and General Science.‖ He paused to emphasize his previous warning. —Do not spend any time on a single question, just mark it and move to the next. You probably won‛t finish all the tests.‖ He then paused, looked at each of us, and said, —Any other questions?‖

We glanced at each other, hoping someone else would show their weakness by asking a question. Nope. We were a motley herd of deer caught in the high beams of an oncoming truck, other than the drunk. He was semi-awake and staring aimlessly out the front windows of the admin building.

I finished all the tests in the time provided except the math test. It was far more challenging than the others. In fact, the others were somewhat of a let-down. I expected something difficult, but they were mostly simple, common-sense questions. Unfortunately, the math portion made up for them. I became physically sick to my stomach. The thought of losing my dream job due to failing the math portion of this test incensed me. I was, for the first time ever, mentally kicking myself over failing to pay attention in school. I am certain my head was shaking as I self-flagellated for being a total, no-load, idiot in school.

When Joe picked up my math test after calling time, I must have looked how I felt, *despondent*. He gave me a concerned look and said, —You don‛t look pleased with how you did on the test.‖

—No, sir.‖ I tried not to reveal I was worried sick as I replied, —I think it was much tougher compared to the others. I didn't finish it.‖ He just smiled and ushered us all back to the reception area for about 45 minutes of additional waiting while he graded the tests.

This may seem insensitive, but I think I know how a man on death row feels in his final minutes. I went to the bathroom three times. My bowels loosened like a malfunctioning soft-serve ice cream machine in the day's heat. I didn't know what I would tell Vangie if I didn't get to interview because of poor test scores. I would probably lie and tell her they changed their minds about hiring anyone today. I was completely sick about the math test. I was certain I had failed it.

After what seemed like hours, Joe returned to the reception area with a serious look on his face. My heart instantly sank when he looked directly at me, void of emotion.

—Everyone *except* Mark Gregg may leave.‖ He then looked toward the others. —Unfortunately, you did not pass one or more of the tests.‖ He paused, and then rhetorically said, —You are eligible to retake these tests in six months, and we welcome you back to do so if you are still interested in the job.‖

A liberating wave of relief swept over me. I couldn't believe it. I even passed the math test. I was stunned, excited, and reeling from Joe's proclamation. He waited for the others to clear the front door of the reception area before continuing.

—You did very well on the tests. He paused and looked at his watch. —The math test was your weakest, but you still did well.‖ His words echoed inside my brain as I tried to grasp that I had even passed the math test.

Joe looked at his watch again. —I need to grab Larry Wood before he heads back into the plant.‖ Joe left the reception area and returned a few minutes later with a man in his mid to late 40s with a cigarette hanging from his mouth. *Don''t they realize those things will kill you?*

—This is Larry Wood. He is our Operations Manager.‖ I stood and shook his hand. He had a friendly smile and acted like he knew me already. —Step into my office, Mark.‖

He turned to Joe and said, —I won't be long. I will have him talk to Joe Montague when I'm done, and then you can have him back.‖ Joe Johnson left as I sat down in Larry's spacious office. He didn't waste any time getting down to business.

—I grew up in Montrose.‖ He again smiled broadly and took a long drag from his cigarette. —After Joe gave me your application, I called my dad to see if he had heard of you. Turns out you have worked on his car for years.‖

—You mean...‖

—Yup... Andy Wood.‖ He smiled broadly while taking another drag from his cigarette. I could then see a bit of resemblance to his old man, but it was obvious he must look more like his mom. I never saw her. I wasn't even sure she was alive as his dad always seemed like a lonely soul.

What a small world. Andy Wood, his dad, was a stodgy but nice old gentleman who drove a Blue 1968 American Motors Ambassador. He was a bit of a pain in the butt, but fortunately, I had always treated him well.

Larry was correct. I had serviced his car for two or three years while working for the filling station and garage in high school. I spent many timely sessions talking to him as I serviced his car. He loved to sit and talk no matter how busy I was. He never mentioned he had a son in the utility industry. Again, I was relieved I had never mistreated him.

—You did very well on the tests.‖ He then took another long drag on his cigarette. —The only question I have is why would you want to leave a beautiful town like Montrose and come to a shit-hole like Rock Springs?‖ He looked genuinely concerned at this juncture. *I was shocked at his characterization of Rock Springs.*

—My Dad works as a Supervisor at the Bureau of Reclamation dispatch center in Montrose, and I have two brothers who both work in steam plants. One is at the Colstrip Plant for Montana Power, and one is at Hayden Station for Colorado Ute Electric Association. I have wanted to work in a power plant since kindergarten.‖ He grinned like he won a million-dollar lottery.

—You couldn't have given me a better answer than that.‖ He paused, and his grin quickly turned to a grimace.

—Rock Springs is just a ***damn NASTY*** place right now. The industrial and mining boom has made this place a hell hole.‖ He paused and looked straight into my eyes. —Are you married?

—Yes,‖ I answered pensively. —She is at the Motel in Rock Springs.‖ I debated in my mind whether to say anything else but continued hesitantly. —We have a baby girl about a month old.‖

His countenance again dropped. He shook his head slowly. —This is a tough place to bring a wife and kid.‖ His countenance lifted slightly before he continued. —However, they are trying to clean it up. We have a new Sheriff named Ed Cantrell. He seems committed to cleaning up Rock Springs.‖ I was panicking. I felt like my dream job was slipping away.

I put my right hand on his desk and leaning slightly forward said, —My wife and I will do fine here. We are both excited about this opportunity.‖ He stared at me for a minute, and his smile edged back.

—I believe you will do well. The opportunity at this plant is unparalleled. As you have probably noticed, we have three units and are building a fourth. You could, conceivably, be a control room operator in 5 to 8 years. They are currently making over $18.50 an hour. The operators here are the highest-paid in the country.‖

—I will work hard and do whatever it takes to learn this job if you give me the chance.‖ I could feel and hear the desperation in my voice.‖

He flashed a look of satisfaction and said, —I want you to speak to Joe Montague, the Plant Manager. If he okays hiring you, I am offering you the job today.‖ I was stunned by this.

With a strained smile, he lowered his voice to almost a whisper. —Joe's a bit different.‖ He paused and took a long, deep drag from his cigarette, turned his head and tried to suppress a cough.

—Just answer his questions honestly, and you'll be fine.‖ He took another hit on his cigarette and then coughed aloud. —Wait here, and I will see if Joe is available.‖

I sat in Larry's office for a bit with my thoughts spinning out of control. How would we come up with the money to move, pay rent, and pay for all the deposits and other expenses?

As I contemplated everything that was happening, Larry came back, put his hand on the door case, and leaned into the office with a look of exasperation. He raised his eyebrows and slowly said, —Joe is available.i Follow me now.‖ Turns out Joe Montague's office was right next door to his. This explains why he lowered his voice a few moments earlier.

—Joe, this is Mark Gregg. I want to hire him for an Operation's Helper job.‖

I carefully extended my right hand towards the older gentleman sitting in the chair. He just stared at me with undisguised angst blanketing his face and then slowly, laboriously reached out to shake my hand. I was mortified at my reception. Joe was at least 60 or so years old. He was bald but had a tight, white strip of hair wrapping from ear to ear around the lower perimeter of his skull. His oversized, square, dark-rimmed glasses were harsh for his pale tincture. He was wearing a white shirt and thin black tie and appeared quite lean and tall, as best I could tell with him sitting down.

I learned later that he was an —up-and-comer‖ at the headquarters of Pacific Power and Light in Portland. Rumors had it that he stepped into a pile of crap (probably due to his abhorrent people skills) and was shipped out to this plant as a punitive measure. I would never know if this was true or not, but it was a rumor that everyone stood by. In those few short moments of meeting him, it was incredibly obvious that he hated Rock Springs and this plant.

Joe barely glanced at my job application and then tossed it carelessly back on his desk, staring angrily at me. —Do you even have a place to live?‖ His voice was laced with impatience, bordering on revulsion. I couldn't tell if it was just me, or having to hire someone rubbing him the wrong way.

I slowly shook my head as I said, —No, sir. I haven't bothered to look because I didn't know whether I was getting this job or not.‖ He openly glared at me for several uncomfortable seconds.

—*WOOD, GET THE HELL IN HERE*!‖ He yelled abruptly, scaring me out of a week's growth. I jumped a few inches at his unrestrained screech. Larry came quickly back to Joe's door with a disgusted look.

Joe continued, —I don't think we should hire him unless he finds a place to live. Now, get him the hell out of here. I am busy.‖

I was staggered by this entire encounter. At 19 years old, I am unsure I had ever dealt with a man this abrupt and rude. Especially not someone in his elevated position.

Fortunately, it was the very last time I ever talked to Joe Montague. In fact, in my entire time at Bridger, I only saw him once out in the plant. He was out by the ash silos prancing like a peacock and talking to himself. It was a bit surreal. He certainly seemed a strange and tormented soul.

—Come on back to my office, Mark.‖ Larry turned and walked back to his office with me in tow. Once in his office, he looked at me with the broad grin he had earlier and, in almost a whisper, said, —Interesting fellow, isn't he?‖

I looked down at the floor for a moment. —Yeah, he is.‖ I wanted to tell him I almost peed myself but knew this would not sound very manly. Larry tilted his head toward his office door and continued.

—We have construction trailers in Rock Springs used by the engineers and managers during construction of the first three units. PP&L wants to close them out, but I checked, and we can get you into one of them.‖ He paused, raised his eyebrows, and took another hit from his cigarette. —That is, if you are interested.‖ He coughed a few more times and continued. —They aren't new, but they are three-bedroom units and work well for their purpose. The big thing is, they are much cheaper than anything else you might find in Rock Springs… If you could even find something, which I doubt you could.‖ He looked slyly at me, leaned towards Joe Montague's office, and smiled. —Again, this is if you want the job and don't mind living in a trailer house.‖

—Absolutely!‖ I quickly replied. —This sounds great to me.‖

—You must get a physical exam because I need you to start here immediately, or sooner if possible… I figured you would say yes to the trailer, so I have you scheduled for a physical exam in about an hour.‖

He paused and looked at his watch. —Do you have any issue with staying the night in Rock Springs and finishing everything tomorrow?‖ He paused, and squinted, and looked directly at me. —I need you to start work as soon as possible.‖

I was completely overwhelmed. —Yes, this works for me.‖ I tried to project an air of confidence even though I was freaked out inside.

He handed me a slip of paper. It was a sloppily written note scribbled with the address of the Doctor's office and another line that said, Cañon Court, Space 27.

—This is the address of the doctor's office and the available trailer. It is in a trailer park on the east side of town. You won't be able to see the interior, but you can at least see where you will be living.‖

—Thank you so much. You don't know how much I appreciate this.‖ I was being honest. I was overwhelmed by everything that had happened in the past hour.

—Believe me, Mark, you will earn every bit of it. Now get into the Doctor's office and get that physical.‖

I left the plant experiencing the highest high and lowest low, trying to reconcile everything that happened that morning while figuring out how we would pull this whole thing off.

~4~
ROCK SPRINGS, HEAD-ON

The Doctor's office in Rock Springs was an aging, double-wide trailer with the external wood veneer peeling in random areas. The parking lot was full, forcing me to park on the street.

Entering the office immediately assaulted my senses by the repulsive odor of dirty gym socks and urine. The waiting room was packed with sick people. There was not an empty seat, and several younger people and kids were sitting on the floor. It reminded me of images of a third world refugee camp on TV.

I pardoned my way over to the receptionist at the desk. She was frazzled and tense. I waited a few minutes while she simultaneously talked to someone at the desk and on the phone.

—My name is Mark Gregg, and I am supposed to get a physical for PP&L.‖

She just looked at me with hollow eyes and said, —Take this and give me a urine specimen.‖ She handed me a Dixie™ cup. No lid, no label, just a standard Dixie™ cup. She pointed to the restroom in the corner of the waiting area as she refocused on another person standing by her desk. I had to wait for a visibly ill man to finish in the restroom. It was not clean and smelled like death or worse. I filled the cup about 3/4 full of my urine and looked for a box, a door, or any place to put it. There was nothing. It was just a small double-wide trailer restroom. Now what?

I exited the restroom and carried the Dixie™ cup back to the front desk, stepping over a couple of kids on the floor and weaving around the adults occupying every available space, all the while trying not to spill the tepid body elixir on anyone.

—What should I do with this? I asked the receptionist in a low voice. From her look, she desperately wanted to tell me what to do with it. However, she practiced restraint.

—Just hold it until the Doctor is ready to see you.

Really? Hold it? I wanted to say something but bit my tongue, knowing that silence was the better part of valor.

I stood there for over 45 minutes, clutching a cup of urine as, one by one, patients were called back to see the doctor. I had to switch hands several times because my arm grew tired, and there was no place to set it down without directly offending someone in this cramped, overcrowded waiting room.

Finally, it was my turn. A weary-looking nurse stepped into the reception area and called my name. I followed her into a small, dingy room with a sink, a cabinet with a half-broken door, a paper towel holder, two worn-out chairs, and an exam table still covered in soiled paper from the previous patient. The condition—and smell—of the place left me in disbelief as I carefully placed the now ice-cold cup of urine on the counter.

Another 15 minutes passed before an elderly man lumbered in, his thinning white hair and oversized bifocals giving him a grandfatherly air. A stethoscope hung loosely around his neck as he made his slow entrance into the room.

—Soooooo, you're here from PP&L for a pre-job physical, huh? His countenance screamed of defeat and fatigue. He looked numb and sounded lifeless.

—Yes, sir. I answered as positively as I could.

—How old are you? His blank stare was uncomfortable.

He looked at me, but I knew he wasn't seeing me.

—19.‖

—Been sick lately?‖

—No, sir.‖

—Had any surgeries in the past few years?‖

—No, sir.‖

He abruptly pulled up the back of my shirt and nailed me with the ice-cold stethoscope. I jumped when the cold steel of the stethoscope hit my warm upper back.

—Reflexes are good!‖ He laughed and coughed a wet, congested cough at the same time.

—Breath hard.‖ I complied and began hyperventilating.

—Enough.‖ He jerked my shirt back down.

—This yours?‖ He grabbed the Dixie™ cup and lifted it to chest level.

—Yes, sir.‖

He tilted the cup slightly, peering at the golden fluid through his bifocals, swirling it like a fine wine in a crystal goblet. He then tossed the contents into the sink and threw the cup in the trash. He was obviously a laboratory savant and could discern all manner of disease with a quick swirl of the cup.

—Get the hell out of here. I got sick people to see.‖ He winked, grinned, and lumbered out of the room. At least there was some partial humanity at the end of my extensive medical review.

I was beginning to realize just how screwed up Rock Springs was. However, I was wrong. It was far, far worse than I could ever imagine at that time. We were in for quite a ride here in Rock Springs. However, it didn't matter. *It was what I had to do.*

I immediately went back to the motel and told Vangie everything that had happened that day. She was getting tense because she hadn't heard from me. I know she was missing Brandi, but being offered the job cleared one hurdle and presented numerous others. In her heart, she now had to reconcile leaving Montrose, family, and bringing our newborn daughter to this place.

I took her hand and said, ‖Let's go look at Rock Springs in the daylight and see the trailer they are renting us.‖ We then jetted off in the Camaro to see our new home.

The trailer court was on the eastern edge of town. It was a 1/8-mile-long strip of aging, damaged asphalt with beat-up, almost identical, beige, single-wide trailer houses parked precariously close to one another.

Each trailer had a small concrete pad by its entrance. Some of the pads had barbecue grills and a chair or two, but most just had trash cans and junk sitting on the pad. Space–27 was one trailer away from the east end. It was a 5 - or 6 -year-old, 12'x 60' aluminum-sided trailer. I didn't know it then, but it was a very low-cost trailer house and only had 3‖ sidewalls.

Sidewalls this thin flexed so badly in the intense Wyoming wind that the front and rear doors would randomly pop open in wind gusts. After moving in, we would wedge a butter knife in the doors to keep them closed.

The flat, tin roof would gallop spectacularly during the constant wind gusts, scaring us all and usually causing Brandi to cry. However, we had a place to live. Had they not rented us this trailer, taking the job would have probably been impossible. As nasty as it was, I was always thankful for that trailer.

Viewing the trailer was the *climax* of our daylight drive through Rock Springs. We drove by the hospital. It was a building of quarried rock construction circa the 1890s and in obvious disrepair. The schools appeared to be of similar vintage and equally sad shape. As we previously observed, the downtown area was riddled with bars and ladies of the night openly parading their —goods‖ on the street.

Vangie had little to say about the town and remained emotionless during our scouting excursion. Looking back, I am certain she was afraid to be negative because I was so gung-ho about the job and moving there.

The following day went very well. The clinic called with the good news that my extensive, super high-intensity medical examination proved me healthy enough for the physical exertion necessary in the plant laborer position. The receptionist and personnel manager at the plant signed me up for benefits and took care of providing the hiring terms and conditions.

I was given a key to the trailer and told the rent would be deducted from my second paycheck every month, but it would not start until we took possession of the home. I could not believe how well everything was coming together.

The final item of business at the plant was determining a start date. I told Larry Wood I would be there immediately after giving my two-week notice of quitting Corelli Auto Sales. I told him we must sell our home, which should sell quickly. Even if it didn‘t, I assured him I would be there after the two-week notice was up.

It was that simple. I was now employed in my dream job. I was officially a power plant worker. Okay, I was a laborer. The journey of a thousand miles begins with the first step. That step was now planted.

~5~
THE FIRST BIG MOVE

My lifelong dream of working in a power plant was now a reality. Against all odds, this high school dropout snagged a position as a laborer at one of the largest coal-fired plants in the entire nation. My starting wage was $4.25 an hour. While barely a living wage in 1976, and being it was in the single largest —boom town‖ in the United States, things were going to be financially stressed (at best). However, I would have taken the job for half that just to get my proverbial „foot in the door."

I vacationed the week Brandi was born at Corelli Auto Sales. I was then forced to take another three days off to interview for the Laborer's position at the Bridger plant.

The three days off for the interview were supposed to be two, but the extra day in Rock Springs caused it to be three. This did not go over well with Emmett Corelli, the owner of the car lot. Between my past screw-ups and missing work for the interview, I returned to a brief but final firestorm at Corelli Auto Sales.

Emmett's son Derrick was a year younger than me, but Emmett was grooming him to run the business. I unlocked the shop early that morning before Derrick or Emmett arrived. I immediately started working on a Chevy pickup that needed U-Joints when Derrick stepped loudly into the shop. I slowly slid out from under the intensely battered farm truck and stood up. Derrick's face was ashen, and his voice was shaking. He had a look of intense disdain, and sheer anxiety on his face. Like his dad, he was usually laid back, sporting a lame smile. The two were carbon copies of each other.

—Where the hell were you yesterday?‖ He was noticeably agitated and shaking.

—Sorry, but I didn't return to town in time to come in yesterday.‖ They did not know I was interviewing at the power plant. I just told them I had personal business out of town.

—Pack your tools and get the hell out.‖ I was immediately stunned and taken aback. I had never been fired before. This was obviously a first for both of us. Based on his tormented demeanor and shaking voice, it was obvious Derrick had never fired anyone.

We just stared at each other for a few moments. My mind was reeling, and I was unsure what to even say to him. One thing I did know, I wasn't asking why. My performance of late was depressing me, so it must be worse for them.

—Okay.‖

That's all I said as I looked into his eyes. I was numbed by the intensity of the moment, and the only thing that came to mind was, —Okay.‖

After a few more moments of being dumbfounded, I quietly asked, —What about my last check?‖

—Just get your shit out of the shop and come back tomorrow.‖ Dad will have a check for you then.

He remained in the shop watching me as I washed my hands and haltingly gathered my tools. We never spoke a single word… *Not one single word*. The 30 or so minutes of silence it took to gather my tools was one of the most awkward and embarrassing things I ever endured. I felt like the biggest loser in the entire world. I was fired on the spot and not even trusted to gather my tools without a witness. My mind was already racing as I tried to think ahead about what I was going to do. We were already broke. This certainly wasn't going to help.

I finished loading the last of my tools into my large, upright, roll-around toolbox while Derrick watched with a scowl. I had a ton of tools. I had been buying them, much of the time, on credit from the tool vendors for a couple of years.

I didn't have a way to get the toolbox from the shop to the house without borrowing a pickup. I certainly wasn't asking Derrick for a truck. I decided I would have to get Dad's pick-up and return later. I locked the toolbox and turned towards Derrick.

—I'll have to borrow my dad's pickup to get the toolbox out of here.‖ I walked over to Derrick and extended my right hand. He looked into my eyes, turned around, and walked back into the office, slamming the door in my face.

That rotten little sonofabitch. I thought I was immature, but this trumped me. However, it was the best thing he could have done. At least now I felt justified about driving away from that place. I didn't ever want to work for someone like him again. Unfortunately, now, I had to face Vangie.

My mind went to high speed as I drove home. I didn't realize it then, but I continuously twisted things to make them seem better than they were. I thought I was fooling Vangie. Fortunately, and unfortunately, the only one being fooled was me. Because of our non-existent courtship and quick marriage, we learned about each other daily. She was learning about me and my ways much faster than I was learning about her.

I walked into the house, gave her a quick kiss, took Brandi out of the bassinet, cuddling her in my arms. She was such a tiny, beautiful little cherub.

—What are you doing home?‖ Vangie asked in a concerned voice.

—As you know, I went in to give my two-week notice today, but Derrick fired me after I gave it to him.‖

I was, of course, lying because I didn't get a chance to give my notice before he fired me. I was very careful to season my voice with ample righteous indignation.

—Why would he do that?‖

She was stunned. I, of course, had not elaborated on just how badly I screwed up some of the recent vehicles I worked on. In fact, I probably led her to believe that I was one of the most gifted mechanics on the face of this earth, possibly in the entire universe. I mean, really, I wanted my amazing wife to think as much of me as possible. Why would I tell her that I was a one-man automotive wrecking team on many of the vehicles I worked-on?

I looked into her golden-brown eyes and shook my head in righteous indignation and said, —They were pissed because I took time off when we were so busy in the shop.‖

She gave me a puzzled look and said, —There had to be more to it than that.‖ She was a smart girl and knew there was more to the story than just missing a few work days.

—Derrick is a jerk!‖ I exclaimed with righteous indignation. —We have never gotten along, and he has a buddy he wants to work there.‖ This was a lie, but I had to come up with something. It's funny how one lie always leads to others.

She gave me an even more puzzled look, bordering on irritation. —You always liked Derrick. When did he become a jerk?‖

Oops. Maybe it's not my most clever lie ever. I should have thought this one over.

—Things have been deteriorating. I just haven't said anything. I knew I had to change the subject. —Besides, I was quitting anyway. What does it matter?

"Maybe we need the money?" She answered sardonically. She wasn't suppressing her dissatisfaction as much as I would have liked. We had bills and were planning a move in just a few weeks. She was correct, as usual; we definitely needed the money.

—I got it covered. We will be fine! The best defense is a good offense? Not really. We had been married long enough that she was already well-versed in my tactics. In a game of verbal fencing, she sported a razor-honed cutlass. I was lucky to wield a dull butter knife when we sparred. Seriously. She reminded me of my dad in this area. He was always one step in front of me, and so was she... Maybe even two or three.

—What are you going to do? As usual, she went straight to the point.

—The house should sell quickly and put some money into our hands. Plus, I can make a loan at the bank to carry us and pay for the move to Rock Springs. I was impressed. This just popped out of my mouth with no forethought, and it sounded pretty good to me.

—Will you make enough money at the power plant to even pay off a loan? She, of course, knew what the plant offered, and we had already talked about it being —tight until I got a raise.

—I think there will be a ton of overtime at Bridger. Plus, we should have a little money left over from selling the house. I would twist anything to my advantage. She was always so darn sensible that it made me work extra hard to sell stupid to her. I would later realize that I rarely —sold stupid‖ to her. She just gave up arguing with my sheer idiocy.

—Whatever.‖ She shook her head with resignation. —You need to do something because we are broke.‖ She was right. I didn't know how much Emmett was paying me tomorrow or even if he would give me a paycheck or not. I hoped so. We really needed it.

I headed back to town, borrowed Dad's pickup, and went to collect my tools. The tension in the air was thick as I walked in. This time, Derrick was nowhere to be seen. Instead, Emmett himself came out to the pickup, his face flushed with anger. Without a word, he handed me a handwritten check, his expression making it clear he wasn't in the mood for conversation. As he turned to leave, I thanked him, but he didn't acknowledge it and just kept walking. The check seemed a little short, but I wasn't about to argue. It was better than nothing.

I was just as surprised by Emmett's behavior as I had been by Derrick's. Both of them handled the situation with a level of pettiness and immaturity that caught me off guard. Despite the mistakes I'd made working for them, I'd always worked hard and, despite the mishaps, done some good work, too.

The next day, I put on the only clean pair of pants and shirt I owned—free of the grease and oil that seemed to magically attach itself to my clothes even from 30 yards away. Feeling as confident as a death row inmate hoping for a last-minute pardon, I walked into the bank and asked for a $1,000 loan to start fresh in Rock Springs, Wyoming. To my relief, they approved the loan, with my tools as collateral. I couldn't believe my luck—I was beyond relieved!

The next couple of weeks were busy with packing and moving preparations. I was starting work at the Bridger plant immediately after Christmas. Dad volunteered himself and his pickup for the move. This was a huge weight off my back because renting a U-Haul *trailer* was far less money than renting a U-Haul *truck*. Dad was certain that a large U-Haul trailer behind his pickup would be enough space to move our meager belongings. Even though I didn't think so then, he turned out to be correct.

There was more good news. A prospective buyer made an offer on our house. It wasn't an excellent offer, but I didn't want to risk the sale not happening. I convinced a very skeptical Vangie we should sign the contract. She was in favor of countering for more money. I probably should have done this, but their first offer gave us enough to pay off the loan at the bank, so I jumped on it.

Christmas arrived very quickly. We spent very little money that year on Christmas presents. Vangie was amazing when it came to money. She was not a spender. She was very careful how she spent *any* of our money. When she did spend money, it was for exactly what was needed at the time. She would always shop for the best prices she could find in every situation. My wonderful little wife was frugal, careful, mature, and certainly not extravagant in her spending practices.

I will never forget saying goodbye to Vangie's folks and loading her and Brandi into the car to leave for Rock Springs. It was snowing lightly in Montrose and was very cold. Vangie was stoic and carefully hugged her folks, getting into the car without shedding a tear. That was always her way. She has been accused of being cold by many people in her life. However, there was not an ounce of coldness in her. She just held her emotions very tightly. Alex and Cordie both cried as they held Brandi for the last time before we left.

As we pulled out of her folk's driveway, she looked at me with her eyes watering a bit. —That was harder than I thought.‖

That was it. She didn't do drama and would go out of her way to avoid it in cases like this. I don't think I truly realized how hard this was for her because she didn't outwardly show it. She was an amazing woman, and it took me years to fully grasp just how much so.

We arrived in Rock Springs much later than anticipated due to the nasty winter weather. We chose to go the long way through Baggs, Wyoming, because the weather in the Utah mountains was almost impassable. Even though we did not have to brave the mountains, it wasn't much better traveling through Baggs due to the wind and driving snow. We were in complete blizzard conditions for the final 3 or so hours.

We arrived at our trailerin Rock Springs completely exhausted. We immediately turned up the heat, securing Brandi in the back bedroom as Dad, Vangie, and I unloaded the U-Haul trailer and the remaining goods in the pickup.

Our new trailer house had cheap, worn-out, gold shag carpeting. Long shag carpeting was a popular thing in 1976. I look back on it now, and it was, frankly, disgusting. The trailer wasn't filthy but was certainly not up to Vangie's standard of cleaning. She was trying to spot clean as we unloaded and haphazardly arranged furniture in the small trailer. Dad was hurrying to return the U-Haul trailer to the U-Haul dealer before they closed that night.

I assumed Dad would return after dropping the trailer and stay the night as it was already late, and the trip here was exhausting due to the weather. However, Dad was never one to let grass grow under his feet.

He announced he was dropping off the U-Haul trailer and then heading back to Montrose… Snow and all. I tried to talk him out of it, but my efforts were a waste of time. His mind was made up. He simply wished us the best and drove away. No fanfare, no hesitation. He didn't even go back and see Brandi before he left. This didn't surprise me. He generally didn't hold grandbabies, toddlers, teens, or young adults in high esteem.

There were three food stores in Rock Springs in 1976. They were Ben's Foodliner, Albertsons, and Safeway. We shopped at the Safeway food store because Ben's was downtown, and downtown Rock Springs was a good place to die on any given day. Am I exaggerating? Not at all.

Reading the local Rock Springs Rocket Miner newspaper revealed a boom town, bursting at the seams, crime-ridden, and full of every conceivable problem associated with rampant growth. The medical community was, at best, awful and, at worst, non-existent. My experience with the physical exam prior to employment was not atypical of any medical treatment. As we found out later, Rock Springs was not a good place to get sick but a potentially quick place to die.

There were continuous accusations of the mafia being fully embedded and functional in the town's life, politics, and day-to-day activities. After I started work, the daily scuttlebutt at the plant convinced me this was all true. From the availability and manufacturing of illegal drugs to the open and flagrant marketing and practice of prostitution on the city streets, the signs of corruption and moral decay were prevalent everywhere you looked in the city.

A few months prior to us moving there in 1978, the new Rock Springs Sheriff, Ed Cantrell, pledged to clean up the town. It seemed he had many controversial practices and policies. His life would later be the subject of an interesting book by his lawyer, Gerry Spence. The book is called —Gunning for Justice.‖ Gerry Spence was an egotistical, high-profile criminal lawyer who never lost a case. This included defending Sheriff Ed Cantrell for shooting to death of one of his undercover drug cops sitting in the back seat of Ed's cop car. After a short argument, Ed turned from the front seat and shot his undercover drug agent right between the eyes.

Rock Springs was a wild and scary place. Being there in the mid to late 1970s was not much different than being in Dodge City, Kansas, or Tombstone, Arizona, in the mid to late 1890s. The only major difference was a vast technological improvement but very little else.

You didn't have to live long in Rock Springs, Wyoming in 1977/1978 to realize it was a hard area unsuitable for soft people. In my mind, all of this was minutia, and really didn't matter. I had my power plant job, and it couldn't get any better than this.

~6~
JIM BRIDGER POWER PLANT

I felt an unsettling combination of both anxiety and excitement my first morning at the plant. The thought of working in one of these massive, mechanical behemoths had me quivering with anticipation. It didn't matter that I was starting as a laborer, I was

Jim Bridger Power Plant circa 1980

finally working in a powerplant.

I had to sit through an hour-long safety lecture that simply stated, —there are a million ways to die in this plant… Be carefull‖. When finished, I was led into the plant by Joe Johnson. It was exhilarating to walk from the admin area into the sweltering cacophony of blaring pumps, turbines, and equipment necessary to convert coal into electricity.

As I entered the power plant, I was immediately overwhelmed by the sights and sounds of the industrial elegance surrounding me. With their graceful, almost lyrical piping, the huge bearing cooling water heat exchangers marked the beginning of a journey through the plant's intricate heart.

The seismic rumble of the coal pulverizers and the ear-splitting roar of the fan rooms left me both awed and humbled. This was a world where every piece of equipment seemed to pulse with life, yet it was also a world of relentless, hard labor. My introduction to this demanding environment was nothing short of exhilarating, but little did I know that my true companion in the months to come would be the lowly shovel, which would soon become my steadfast ally in the daily grind of shoveling ash—a task that would test my endurance and determination like nothing else.

The problem in so many of these plants, including Bridger, was the bottom and flyash handling systems were poorly designed maintenance nightmares, almost impossible to keep in service. *Could it be because these systems were forced to handle over 400 tons of wet, abrasive ash per hour?* The bottom and fly ash hoppers plugged continuously causing ash to build up in the hoppers, forcing the plant personnel to either shut down the plant or dump the ash on the floor.

Typically, they would dump tons of ash onto the floors of the plant. So much ash was being dumped on the floors that plant personnel used makeshift plywood barriers to keep the ash away from the major pieces of equipment. And… This is where I came into the mix.

Joe Johnson took me to the tool crib near the maintenance shop, checked out a shovel, and then walked me over to the bottom ash area. Several laborers were already shoveling the hot, dense bottom ash into green dumpsters.

I had no idea how quickly the abrasive, sharp ash would blister my hands from the continuous death grip on the shovel. This was made worse by perpetually wet gloves.

Continuously shoveling dense, wet bottom ash in the dingy, sweltering bowels of a power plant exhausts even the fittest individual in just a few hours. Coming back day after day, after day, after day after day, and shoveling this same ash exhausts your soul and virtually robs you of the will to live. Exaggeration? Try it for a couple of weeks... *Make your own decision.* Fortunately, there were some breaks. Unfortunately, the breaks were called flyash.

Only part of the ash in a coal-fired plant is bottom ash. The coal is ground to the consistency of face powder in the pulverizers and blown into the furnace burning in suspension. The heavier constituents in the fuel agglomerate and fall into the bottom ash hoppers, but the rest is carried out of the boiler as flyash.

Flyash resembles fluffy talcum powder but is light gray and velvety. It flows and splashes like water and even pours like water. If you fall into a silo filled with flyash, it is akin to falling into a tank of water, except you sink quickly, much like you would in thin quicksand.

If left in the ash silo for an extended time, your body would quickly dissolve due to the moisture content of your body reacting to the sulfur compounds in the ash, producing acid and consuming your bodily tissue. None of this was explained to us as we worked in and around the silos, much of the time with the access doors open.

A laborer's break from bottom ash was... *FLYASH*. Yup. I did so well day after day shoveling bottom ash that I was given periodic breaks from shoveling bottom ash to shovel, chip, and vacuum flyash. The part I am leaving out is the favor I was gaining with Joe Johnson and other supervisors. This favor was incredibly important.

Every six months, the plant opened a power plant operations training class. They would test and then pick five or six of the most promising laborers who passed the testing to enter this class. There was about a $2.00 per hour pay increase, and you sat for 40 hours a week for 4 or 5 months and learned how to operate this amazing mechanical wonderland. To me, this was the GRAND PRIZE and worth every blister and uncomfortable, sweltering, noisy day in the plant.

It only took a few days on the job before I began automatically volunteering for any special duty when asked. Usually, when they asked for a volunteer, it was a total crap job. Didn't matter. I volunteered for everything. However, it started working to my advantage. They became aware that I would automatically volunteer any time they asked. They started mixing some of the crap jobs with the easy jobs, like driving a pick-up to Rock Springs to retrieve something from town or driving to the water pumping station in Green River to clean, there.

My volunteering provided good and not-so-good experiences. One of my worst experiences from unquestioningly volunteering was finding out I was to manually unplug the sewage treatment plant drain culvert.

The plant had its own on-site sewage treatment facility. Between construction on unit – 4, and the approximately 275 regular employees on units 1, 2, and 3 there was a lot of raw sewage. It seems that the concrete culvert from the sewage plant to the effluent pond became plugged. Can you guess what it was plugged from? Much of it was mud that backed up from a flooded effluent pond. However, a fair amount of it was not just mud, based on the smell alone.

I was a small, skinny guy who could go into the culvert on my hands and knees and dig out the 10 or 12 linear feet of pluggage. Lovely. It stunk so bad I emptied the contents of my stomach and then dry heaved until getting somewhat acclimated to the repulsive odor.

On one of my entries into the culvert, I had a couple of (union) plant mechanics tell me I shouldn't be in there because I could pick up a horrible disease or sickness due to not wearing proper gear. Damn, union-guys. What was their deal? I had proper gear... I was wearing jeans and a T-shirt, work boots, and gloves. *What more do you need to crawl around in raw sewage???*

The real saving grace of the Operations Helper job was the upgrade and overtime. Because the plant was a union plant, anytime I operated a forklift or other piece of equipment, such as a Bobcat, I would get —upgrade pay. It was $6.60 an hour. A Bobcat is a small bucket loader, sometimes called a _skid-steer.' It is called this because steering this handy little loader was done by locking the two left or two right tires while the other side continued to turn. This would skid the tires and force the loader to turn. Therefore, whenever you filled a small green dumpster using your shovel, you would have to move and dump it using a forklift. A single, 5-minute (or less) trip from the bottom ash area to the random dump area outside the plant would get you 15 to 30 minutes of upgrade pay.

On the few days the Bobcat was available, you would use it to pick up and carry the ash out of the bottom ash area. More upgrade. It helped enhance the meager paychecks enough to pay the bills.

Upgrades and overtime were constant. If you wanted it, overtime was always available—there was always something that needed cleaning somewhere. I never turned down the opportunity. Not only did you get paid time and a half for the extra hours, but you also received a meal ticket as an added bonus.

A meal ticket was a union-mandated slip of paper redeemable for $4.50 worth of food if you worked more than two hours beyond your normal shift. The meal ticket was honored at several local restaurants in Rock Springs. Our favorite was the Sands. It was the Chinese restaurant closest to our trailer park and the one we ate at during the interview process.

The participating restaurants were supposed to only allow the PP&L employee and no one else to eat from the meal-tickets. From day – 1, the waitresses at the Sands allowed Vangie and I to eat using the meal ticket because our total bill was never more than the allotted $4.50. Yes, in 1977/1978, Vangie and I could each have a nice Chinese dinner, and the total cost, including the tip, would not exceed $4.50.

Due to the continuous overtime, we ate at the Sands at least 4 nights per week. If it wasn't occupied, we would sit at our favorite booth and put Brandi's baby carrier on the seat next to Vangie. Brandi was usually a doll. The Asian waitresses would fawn over her as they took our order and delivered the meal.

After a few weeks of eating there regularly, the waitresses began taking Brandi back to the kitchen while we ate. The first time, Vangie and I both freaked out. So much so that after a few minutes of them having her, Vangie walked back to the kitchen. We desperately wanted to ensure that she did not become the stir-fry special for that evening. Vangie found the cooks and waitresses playing with Brandi and keeping her company.

We eventually got comfortable with them taking her to the kitchen when they weren't busy. It gave us an occasional chance to enjoy dinner with just each other.

The new wore off quickly. My hands toughened like shoe leather, and the combination of the intense physical activity and the steady diet of greasy food started packing bulk on my previously gaunt frame. Life was starting to slip into a rut.

~7~
ADJUSTING TO A NEW WORLD.

Life in the trailer park was difficult. Parties or domestic disturbances, or parties with domestic disturbances, happened with predictable regularity. Several entry-level personnel from the plant lived in the park, along with a substantial number of drillers and miners. The drillers seemed to be the wildest of the bunch. However, the powerplant people weren't far behind. Some nights and weekends, the power plant workers took top billing in the noise department.

Our next-door neighbor, Robert Mendara, worked in the oil patch as a well-logger. Not even sure what this was. He used electronic equipment and did diagnostic work of some sort at oil wells. He was quite intense and different from most of the others in the park. Every time we talked, he would bluntly tell me that someday he would own a well-logging company and be a rich oil magnate. I never doubted for a minute that he was serious about this. You could not be as intense and driven as he was without dying of stress or making a fortune. Oddly enough, a few years later, he made his fortune and, in fact, owned a large, lucrative, well logging company.

I helped Bob work on his car and his pick-up. They were in poor shape, and I was far more mechanically inclined and experienced than him. I spent several hours keeping his vehicles running. He never offered to compensate me, and I never asked. However, he continuously exclaimed that —he owed me.‖ He always added that he would —make it right‖ when he was rich and famous. You bet, Bob. I will send you pictures from the moon when I become an astronaut. Even though he was eccentric, we got along well, and he seemed nice. We kept in touch for many years. It was a good thing. He helped us out of a jam a few years later.

Because of our indebtedness and the low pay, my —treat‖ each paycheck was to go grocery shopping with Vangie and get myself a quart of beer and a small jar of pickled pig's feet. What can I say? If you have a gourmet pallet, you naturally choose gourmet food and beverage, *right?* Dad always taught me that poor people have poor ways. I didn't understand it at the time, but I now realize how much sense it really made.

Life was becoming a continuous and depressing grind. I was working too much overtime just to make ends meet, and there was very little to look forward to in Rock Springs other than the possibility of getting into the plant training class.

I would make excuses to go into the control room at every opportunity. At Bridger, the first three units were in one control room. I loved my brief excursions to view the controls and the

Jim Bridger Control Room (Used By Permission)

operators running the plant.

Was I shallow? Obviously. However, I believe most people have an open desire to do something or be somebody specific. Sometimes, this is based on their strengths or inclinations, and sometimes on pure, vain imagination.

I never once considered doing anything else. The powerplant environment was intertwined with my soul and spirit. My only goal in life was eventually making it to the plant's control room. At that time, this was nirvana or heaven. It kept me moving forward daily in the face of shovel-induced madness.

Several grinding months passed on the Rock Springs hamster wheel. Overtime, meal tickets, and more overtime. Life was truly a non-ending monotone of drab consistency.

This consistency was rocked by an unexpected change. One evening, after arriving home late while eating our nightly meal-ticket dinner at the Sands, Vangie looked at me with a concerned look. —I'm late with my period.‖ She paused. —I may be pregnant.‖

I was surprised, maybe even a little shocked.

—Really?‖ I slowly replied. I always had a way with words.

—I haven't said anything because I wanted to go to the Doctor first.‖ She turned and looked at Brandi, who was starting to fuss a bit. —I called the doctor's office and made an appointment to get checked… Her voice trailed off. —I have been waking up sick to my stomach.‖

—Wow,‖ I said in a measured tone. *I was truly a wordsmith at this moment.*

—That's it? Wow?‖ She became irritated. —Nothing else?‖

—No, no, I didn't mean it that way. It is just a surprise.‖ I tried to sound abnormally upbeat. In fact, I really wasn't upset, just genuinely surprised. Unfortunately, she wasn't happy with my comeback.

—Are you pissed or something?‖ She prodded. She was now definitely irritated. I just wanted to run and hide. I knew that no matter what I said or did, this was NOT going to end well.

—No, not at all!‖ I gave her a smile of reassurance. —We never intended Brandi to be an only child. I don't have a problem with this.‖

She stared at me angrily for a moment. —You better deal with it because if I am pregnant, it is a reality.‖

—Seriously, I am good with it…Honest When is your doctor's appointment?‖

—Thursday morning.‖ She turned and rummaged for Brandi's bottle in the diaper bag. I could tell she was irritated with my response and had said all she would say about it for now.

Thursday rolled around. As suspected, the Doctor's visit confirmed her suspicion. She was not —late‖, she was with child.

To say we were both surprised is a huge understatement. However, we were not upset. Brandi was only 8 months old, and 8 months was not a long time between pregnancies. We weren't planning to have another so quickly.

We fully embraced her pregnancy and hoped it would be a boy. We talked at length and decided that if it were a boy, we would name him Joshua David. Little did we know then that we would eventually have our Joshua David, just not this way.

A few weeks after learning she was pregnant, we were in bed, asleep. Our bedroom was in the front of the trailer, directly by the main road in the trailer park. I awakened with a start as Vangie shook my arm.

—Mark, listen...‖ I was reluctantly extracting myself from slumber when the oddest noise came into focus. It was a loud, intermittent hissing, followed by maniacal laughter. My body tensed, and I cocked my head to hear better. Silence. My muscles just started to relax when there was an even louder hissing noise, again followed by a man laughing hysterically. I quickly jumped from bed and looked out the small mobile home window on the front of the trailer.

Across the street and three trailers down I could see a large man with curly, bushy hair leaning down in front of a car tire. He thrust a large knife into the tire of the car. The tire hissed angrily as the air rushed out. The man jumped up, laughing hysterically. I watched as he went to the rear tire of the same car and repeated his actions. Lights were beginning to illuminate around the trailers near the man.

I quickly donned my robe and grabbed the unloaded 22 caliber rifle my brother Wylie had given me years earlier. I always kept it in the bedroom in case we needed it.

I slipped my shoes on without tying them and ran out in front of the trailer. The big man had worked up to another trailer and was still repeating the same bizarre actions. He reminded me of a wild animal violently ripping the flesh from its prey. As soon as he slashed the tire, he would leap up and shake his head violently, his bushy hair slapping his face as he laughed hysterically. Our next-door neighbor exited his trailer the same time as me.

—I called the cops!‖ He exclaimed, cautiously approaching the large, crazed man. He apparently wasn't worried because he saw I had my rifle pointed safely at the lunatic.

With the *unloaded* .22 rifle pointing at the large, disheveled man, I carefully said, —You just hold still for a few minutes.‖

He appeared to be in his early 20's. He was wearing a green army jacket with several large, bulging pockets and was wearing round, wire-frame glasses. His eyes were dull and lifeless, reminding me of the artificial eyes used by a taxidermist. He didn't blink and appeared oblivious to the rifle pointing directly at him. Vangie cautiously walked up and stood by my side.

He stared at me for a few moments and then carefully reached inside his jacket and very slowly, purposely removed a large, nickel-plated revolver. It looked huge, and I had no question that his gun was loaded.

Turning the shiny silver hand cannon directly towards us, he drolly stated, —Let's see who hits the ground first.‖

I could not believe my eyes. I turned toward Vangie and yelled, —RUN!!!"

I grabbed her arm and sprinted toward our trailer, every muscle in my body bracing for the searing pain of a bullet tearing through me—or worse, hitting my pregnant wife. As we neared the corner of the trailer, I quickly glanced back and caught sight of the gun-wielding maniac darting across the street between two trailers before vanishing into the shadows. He was never seen again.

Luckily, the police department showed up about 45 minutes later. Their response was wholly underwhelming. They said they would —keep their eyes open‖ and then told us to go back to bed.

I learned a lesson that night. Never point an unloaded gun at anyone. I've often wondered if I would have shot him had I been properly armed with a loaded rifle. I sincerely doubt it. I think, loaded or not, I would have run just like I did. Unfortunately, my already waning opinion of Rock Springs just took another hit. This place was indeed a nasty place to live.

~8~
THE SKIDSTEER AND THE HOLE IN THE WALL.

I was getting highly adept at shoveling ash. Continuously shoveling, coupled with the abrasion factor in the ash, was turning my hands to sand-impregnated leather. I was careful how I picked up Brandi because my hands were so rough and harsh, they would irritate her skin and make her cry.

The coveted Bobcat or _skid-steer' loader was on its death bed. A total lack of maintenance and continuous use in wet, grinding ash took its toll, and the Bobcat was down for the count. Besides the upgrade pay, the Bobcat saved countless hours of shoveling. In a quick ten-minute period, the Bobcat could do more than 10 men in an hour. We seriously needed the Bobcat, but it was now another example of a completely overwhelmed, uncaring, largely unskilled maintenance force.

It was a common view held by the operators that the mechanical maintenance department consisted primarily of low-life, semi-skilled, whining, union, rabble-rousers. Unfortunately, I shared this opinion.

I didn't know much about anything, but it seemed that most of the Bridger maintenance personnel could not repair their way out of a wet paper sack.

The plant operators at Bridger used to say that the plant mechanics were —*inflicting maintenance*‖ on the equipment and that it would never be the same when they were complete. Even in my vast ignorance, it appeared that this was a true statement.

The mechanics required multiple personnel to do any single job, and they would not pick up or clean ANYTHING when they finished —inflicting maintenance‖ on something. They would even leave tools, large and small, basic or exotic, lying in the ash and on the floors without regard to their cost or condition.

No matter the urgency of any job. They never missed a coffee break (unless offered overtime), and their breaks never finished early. Even though the operators and maintenance personnel were part of the same union, they absolutely hated each other.

The failed Bobcat caused Joe Johnson and a couple of the other supervisors to complain to the maintenance supervisors about their lack of caring and proper maintenance on everything in the plant, including the Bobcat. This further inflamed hostilities between the departments.

The maintenance and operations supervisors openly antagonized and angrily mocked each other. Their issues quickly bled down to the mechanics, and they, at some point, assured Joe Johnson that the Bobcat would *NEVER* be fixed.

Fortunately, Joe Johnson was a resourceful former hillbilly from Oklahoma. He ruminated long and hard (at least a couple of minutes) to hatch an ill-conceived plan with me at the center of it. He asked me into the shift supervisor's office and closed the door to initiate his incredibly flawed scheme.

—Mark, you used to do mechanic work, right?‖ He was fumbling a cigarette in his fingers as always. His southern drawl was more pronounced when he was under duress.

—I did,‖ I said, nodding my head. —I worked in a couple of garages fixing cars and pickups,‖ I answered carefully, wondering where this was headed.

—Do you think you could repair the Bobcat given some time and the necessary tools?‖ He squinted and took a long draw on his cigarette. His hand was visibly shaking. His question caught me off guard. The union situation was extremely strained, and they played hardball in every conflict. If I were caught doing maintenance work, there would be an immediate grievance filed, and the company and I would have to pay for the indiscretion of —stealing‖ work from them.

—I'm sure I could fix it.‖ I answered confidently. My confidence was always highest when I was the most ignorant about something.

Joe leaned closer to me. He always reeked of cigarette smoke, but it was overwhelming at this proximity. His breath was a toxic mixture of excess coffee, rancid cigarette smoke, and maybe a hint of yesterday's lasagna.

He said as he smiled malignantly. —I am trusting you on this.‖ He took a long drag from his cigarette. —A couple of the other Supervisors and I found a way into the tool room. If we can get the tools, would you be willing to fix the Bobcat on the sly?‖ He paused and took *another* drag from his cigarette, flicking the burning ash on the floor. —If we need parts, we can get the warehouse to order them.‖

Again, I didn't even give it much thought. —I'll do it.‖ I laughed a nervous laugh. —I could use the upgrade pay if we get it running again.‖

Joe gave me an impatient courtesy laugh, stood up, and said, —Follow me.‖

We left the Shift Supervisor's office and took the elevator to the plant basement. We went to the crane bay between Unit – 1 and Unit – 2. The huge maintenance shop with the lathes, drill presses, milling machines, and other large machine equipment was located here. The tool room was on the west side of the maintenance shop. It wasn't so much a room as a fenced-off area within the maintenance shop.

The fence was an 8' high chain-link fence with the maintenance shop cinderblock wall as its back wall. There were three sides of the chain-link fence, with the fourth side, or backwall, being the sidewall of the maintenance shop.

When you were in the maintenance shop, you couldn't see inside the tool room because there were tons of straps, chain falls, ropes, electrical extension cords, air hoses, water hoses, and other paraphernalia hanging from the fencing. This blocked the view of the bounty inside the tool room.

The heavier tools and equipment were hanging from the cinderblock back wall. The back wall also had shelves on the lower portion the entire length of the tool room. Overall, the tool room was a congested mess. Like so many other areas in the plant, the Toolroom was poorly organized and maintained.

Unfortunately, the tool room was manned. The maintenance department's utter and complete disregard for expensive tools forced management to man the tool room during dayshift to check out/in the tools. They hoped it would force responsibility and accountability on the mechanics.

I can assure you that, up to this point, untold thousands of dollars of tools were left to rot or be stolen or discarded in the plant every month. Theft from the plant was continuous and, from what I saw and heard, easy to do. Therefore, a young man of Polish descent named Nick Malkovitch was posted at the tool-room French door with a makeshift desk to check out the tools.

Joe and I walked from the elevator amidst the constant din of the plant equipment to the unit – 1 and 2 crane bay. Empty barrels that once contained hydraulic oil, turbine oil, and other lubricants were sloppily stored here. Wouldn't you know it? Behind these barrels, the mortor located between some of the cinderblocks had, somehow, _fallen out.'

Joe looked at me with a look of mirth and mischief on his face. —The back-shift operators occasionally need tools and seem to have engineered a way to get them.‖ He grinned as he bent down and ran his hand carefully across the molested blocks.

He then pulled a large pocket-knife out of his faded blue jeans and started poking and wiggling out the first cinderblock. My eyes were wide with disbelief as, one by one, he pulled three blocks out. There was no doubt that these blocks had been in and out many times in the past.

No one could see us outside the maintenance shop because we were behind the stacked oil barrels. No one could see us inside the maintenance shop because the compromised cinderblocks were on the back side of a bottom shelf that had tools sitting on it. It was a near-perfect plan for stealthy tool extraction.

Joe finished making the hole large enough for me to shimmy through. He then pulled me away from the opening and put his face to my ear so I could hear him above the noise of the plant equipment.

—The hand tools you need are on the left side after you get into the pen. Get what you need, and get the hell out. *DON'T GET CAUGHT!"*

My stomach rolled tightly into a semi-rigid ball, and my thoughts reeled out of control… What? Don't get caught? *There are potentially angry men inside there looking to kill people like me!*

—Good luck!‖ He then broadly grinned, revealing his tobacco-stained teeth. —If you get caught, I will disavow all knowledge of you!‖ This was an obvious reference to the T.V. show called ‗Mission Impossible'. At the beginning of each episode, a tape recorder with the current mission would always end by telling the spy that if they were caught, the government would disavow all knowledge of them.

Wow! This was comforting. I have a wife and baby and another on the way. This was not how I saw my day progressing. As I was catastrophizing, Joe put his hand on my neck, interrupting my thoughts, and pushed me through the clandestine hole in the wall.

I wriggled through the barely large enough hole and onto the bottom shelf containing large wrenches. I had to move the large impact wrenches to get onto the shelf. Nothing stealthy about that. There were a couple of aisles in the tool room that were formed by free-standing shelves placed squarely in the middle of the tool room. Because of this, I couldn‗t see the tool-room attendant but knew he was probably out front by the French door.

I slid off the shelf onto the cold, unforgiving concrete floor, jarring my shoulder, and then quickly made my way to the north side of the tool room. My lack of formal training as a ninja was apparent.

Sure enough, there were big toolboxes filled with hand tools, precisely like Joe said. I glanced to see if the tool room attendant was up front. He was. Luckily, he appeared to be talking to a mechanic.

As quietly as possible, I began opening the toolbox drawers, one by one, grabbing screwdrivers, various size wrenches, and a 3/8 socket set in a plastic carrying case. I grabbed all the tools I felt I could carry and still get out of the cinderblock hole.

I then whipped around to head back to our stealth entrance only to look straight into the eyes of the tool-room attendant and a mechanic standing 2' from me.

Not just any mechanic. An ex-Los Angeles cop named Barry King. He was a muscle-bound Neanderthal. He was mean, loud, obnoxious, and had a 5:00 shadow at 9:00 in the morning. I sat many days in the lunchroom trying to eat my lunch, listening to this loudmouth tell inflated lies about the glory days when he was a cop in L.A.

He was one of the individuals that were always complaining about how badly PP&L was screwing them. As with Nick, the tool room attendant, he didn't look amused that I was borrowing their tools.

—Let's kill him and dump his body in the effluent pond, Barry said as he stared loathingly at me. —This little scab-rat laborer has it coming.

I was scared. While I didn't really think they would kill me, I knew they could rough me up and make me hurt.

—So, you're the little bastard stealing all our tools! He grabbed my arm hard and jerked my 160-pound frame up to his gargantuan chest.

—I have never stolen anything from here! I exclaimed loudly. —This is my first time in the tool room.

—Bullshit! He scowled as he again violently jerked and then let go of my arm, turning and walking to the front of the tool room.

He yelled loudly out into the maintenance shop. —Hey, Tork and Gill, get the hell over here! We gotta situation to deal with.‖

I didn't know whether to run for the door or wet my pants. I may have done the latter, but I would never tell. Two mechanics followed him back to where I was standing.

Barry yelled squarely in my face, —Why are you stealing our tools?‖

—I was getting tools to fix the Bobcat, I was not stealing anything.‖ I replied defiantly.

—Fix the Bobcat?‖ He looked scathingly at the others and back at me. —Who the hell do you think you are?‖

He grabbed my lapel and pulled me to his face. He was a walking muscle, reminiscent of pictures I had seen of the evolutionary missing link. —If you wanna be a *$#@ing mechanic, then bid the job and do the damn apprenticeship!‖ He was screaming directly in my face. —Don't you ever try and do our jobs again, or you will be one sorry little mother*$#@er.‖ He shoved me back away from his face and continued angrily. —We are going to grieve this with the management, but first, we will teach you not to *$#@ with mechanics.‖ He was clearly relishing my shame. Fortunately for me, they had more mischief in their eyes than hatred.

He turned to the tool room attendant. —Nick, get me some duct tape!‖ Nick was wide-eyed and, like me, unsure of what would happen.

Barry grabbed my arm again. —I think we should give this little shit-head some time to think about his sins before we rat on him.‖ Nick quickly returned with four rolls of industrial gray duct tape.

—Guys, I won't do this again!‖ I pleaded as manly as possible. —Just let me go. I can assure you I have learned my lesson.‖ Trying to appeal to their reasonable side was like convincing a fat man that fried chicken tastes bad. In the moment's excitement, it slipped my mind that these guys were the —maintenance inflictors.‖ Frankly, I think their combined IQs were less than one stupid person.

Barry laughed sardonically. —Hell yes you have learned your lesson… We are just helping you remember it forever.‖

I was finding it hard to believe this was a man who once pledged —to protect and to serve.‖ No one I knew ever asked why he quit being a cop and came to the powerplant as a mechanic. It was becoming obvious to me now. They must have imposed some minimum intelligence test that he couldn't pass. I, of course, never said this to his face. I am sure he would have lost the look of mischief, and I would have been inspecting the bottom of the effluent pond.

The duct tape hissed loudly as they ripped it from the rolls to mummify me. They started at my feet and encased me to my neck. They weren't gentle, either. The tape was tight and overlapped several times. I could barely breathe, let alone move.

They picked me up and carried me through the maintenance shop, with most of the mechanics laughing hard at the spectacle of it all.

Barry ripped a chunk of cardboard off a box and wrote, —SCAB-RAT‖ on it. They carried me out to the main piping aisle on Unit – 1 and leaned me against a beam, using one last chunk of duct tape to hang the sign on me. *Yes, they leaned me against a beam.*

This is where it gets humiliating. Word immediately ripped throughout the plant that I was mummified. Everyone in the plant wanted to enjoy my predicament with me. They were coming in droves and laughing. However, it got even worse.

Joe Johnson came and took one look, cracked up laughing, and LEFT ME THERE while rushing over to the plant paging system and calling the day-shift, shift supervisor to come and see me. All in all, I leaned against the beam for over 30 minutes until it was no longer a novelty to anyone.

It took Joe and the day-shift supervisor about 5 times as long to cut me out of my mummification garb as it did to put me there.

Joe was apologetic and asked if I had mentioned his involvement in this hare-brained little scheme. I assured him that I hadn't. He then told me to take a break, and then go shovel some ash on unit – 3.

Apparently, my adventure wasn't for naught. The next day, Barry and one other mechanic started working on the Bobcat. Two days into it, they loaded the gutted Bobcat on a flatbed and took it to town to get fixed properly. One look at the belts, clutches, and hydraulics made me realize I was lucky I didn't get to work on it. Screwing it up may have been more humiliating than the mummification.

A few weeks later, they retrieved the Bobcat from town, running like a new one. All in all, it was certainly worth it. The laborers were able to get an hour of upgrade for 10 minutes' worth of time on it, and a substantial amount of ash was being moved again. It's funny how some things just seem to work out.

~9~

HOSPITAL HELL

Several weeks later, I arrived home from the plant late one evening because I had been working overtime.

I walked into the trailer, and one look at Vangie sent a shiver down my spine. She was pale, and her hair wasn't fixed. Vangie always took immaculate care of herself and the kids. When I saw her countenance, I knew something was wrong. She never did anything before making certain she looked —presentable.‖

—I've been cramping and spotting all day.‖ Her voice was weak, and her eyes sunk in.

—What does that mean? I wasn't sure what —spotting‖ meant.

—I'm bleeding and cramping.‖ I could see then she was worried. You must remember that Vangie is a rock. She is one of the strongest people I have ever met. In fact, it is safe to say she has always been strong to a fault.

—Should I get you to the hospital?‖ I was freaking out on the inside.

—I think I am okay if it doesn't get worse.‖ She did not seem certain, and this scared me. She could have a 104° fever and barely be able to walk, and you would never know it. She would just keep moving forward. It was her nature. I knew this was more serious than she was letting on.

Vangie put Brandi to bed and went to the bathroom. She was there for a while before I heard her faintly call for me. I went to the bathroom door. Her voice was weak, strained, and halting. —Get

Brandi out of her crib.‖ She paused a few moments. I strained to hear her as her voice was muffled and labored. —You've got to take me to the hospital.‖

—Are you okay? Do I need to come in and help you?‖ I spoke rapidly while trying to be calm, but I was not doing well.

—Just get Brandi ready to go.‖ There was a tiny bit of irritation in her voice, I call it the _Latina fire'. This was a good sign. I got Brandi out of her crib and changed her diaper. She was such a sweet girl and barely fussed. She was almost always cheerful, even as a small baby.

Vangie came out of the bathroom looking terrible. She was white as a sheet and seemed unsteady. I helped her to the car and then grabbed Brandi and strapped her into the baby seat. We went straight to the Sweetwater Memorial Hospital.

The hospital was built in 1892 and appeared largely unchanged since its original construction. It was old, dark, and foreboding. The emergency room looked newer than the rest of the hospital but still assaulted your senses with the odor of urine covered by harsh antiseptic. I had Brandi in one arm and helped Vangie with the other into the emergency room.

Our reception nurse at the E.R. was cold and sterile. Vangie told her she was pregnant, cramping, and bleeding badly. The nurse put her on a gurney, wheeled her into a separate enclave, and coldly told me Brandi was not allowed in the emergency room for her own safety. She directed us to a waiting room out in the old portion of the hospital.

—When and how will I know something?‖ The impatience in my voice was obvious.

—We will let you know when we know something. Please go to the waiting area.‖ She appeared entirely disinterested and emotionless. Maybe she was having a bad night, but you would think that becoming a nurse partially entailed being even mildly empathetic. She had the empathy of an unpainted, cold cinderblock.

I walked down the hall to the waiting area, shocked at the age and poor upkeep of the facility. It reminded me of a two-story prison out of an old black-and-white movie. The most shocking thing was the bathrooms. It appeared that there were only two bathrooms per floor, one on each end of both floors. Sick or injured people either walked a sizable distance to a shared toilet or used a bedpan.

I wondered if they even had indoor toilets in 1892. The only hospital I had any experience with was Montrose Memorial Hospital and it seemed centuries newer and substantially nicer than this mausoleum.

After hearing nothing for a couple of hours, I could not keep Brandi in the waiting room much longer. She was getting fussy, and I had already fed her the bottle I brought from home.

I went back to the emergency room. This time, it was a different nurse. She was younger and appeared to be more human than the first nurse. Of course, the first nurse didn't set the bar very high.

—Ma'am, can I get a status update on my wife? Her name is Vangie Gregg. She came in a couple of hours ago with cramps and bleeding.‖ Her countenance immediately dropped. Her expression said volumes without speaking.

—She is resting right now.‖ She said, looking down the emergency room hall. —The doctor is busy but will talk to you as soon as he is free.‖

—Is she okay? My stomach tightened, and I felt sick. —Is everything okay?

—Your wife is fine. She then lowered her voice and gave me a sympathetic look. —The doctor will be out in a bit to talk to you. I was frustrated. I knew with certainty that something was wrong.

The next 30 minutes was hell on earth. I didn't know what to think or what to do. Brandi had fallen back asleep, so I couldn't direct my attention to her. It left me with plenty of time to catastrophize. I had to go to the bathroom several times in those 30 minutes due to my nervous stomach. The bathrooms bore clear and revolting evidence of being used by everyone on that floor.

The nurse came to the waiting area after what seemed like ages. —Mr. Gregg, the Doctor wants to speak to you and your wife together. She is awake now. Please follow me.

With Brandi in my arms, I followed the nurse back to the emergency room where Vangie rested. She was on a roller bed now and not a gurney. The Doctor followed us into the room and sat gingerly on a stool with his arms resting in his lap. He was a disheveled middle-aged man and looked exhausted and gray. He didn't waste any time. He turned the stool and looked directly at Vangie.

—Mrs. Gregg, I am very sorry, but you have had a miscarriage. He then turned towards me. The stool screeched loudly as he pivoted on it. You could tell he was jaded to the point of being numb when delivering bad news. —These things happen, and often times we have no idea why.

It was a surreal moment for us. Vangie was barely showing, and I am unsure his proclamation fully registered in my brain. We had already decided that if it were a boy, his name would be

Joshua David. Other than this, I had not thought much about the baby yet. I was sad, confused, and not entirely sure what I was feeling. I put my hand softly on Vangie's arm and addressed the Doctor.

—Will Vangie be okay?‖

He mechanically nodded his head yes and continued. —She needs a short surgical procedure called a D & C. Dr. Wierman, our local OB/GYN Doctor, has agreed to do it in the morning.‖

Vangie's normally piercing eyes were half closed, tired, and had dark bags under them. However, when he mentioned —surgical procedure‖, they widened, and she turned her head and looked directly at the Doctor.

—What is a D & C?‖ I felt bad for her. It was obvious that this had been a far worse ordeal than she would ever let on. Her toughness always shielded her real feelings.

—D & C stands for dilation and curettage.‖ He seemed distant and simply reciting a memorized script. —It is a procedure necessary when a miscarriage occurs in the first trimester of a pregnancy. It is a simple, relatively fast procedure. Dr. Wierman has done hundreds of them. You will be admitted to the hospital this evening and have the surgery in the morning. If everything goes as expected, you should be discharged tomorrow afternoon.‖ He then stood up and, for the first time, showed a bit of emotion. —I am very, very sorry. The nurse will take care of admitting you to the hospital. If there are no other questions, I must see other patients.‖

I turned to him and with sincerity said, —Thanks for taking care of her.‖ I waited to see if Vangie had anything to say, but she just lay silently.

We sat and stared at each other for a few minutes. Vangie teared up but did not outright cry. I was dazed and just held her hand. Our few moments of mourning were interrupted by the nurse coming back into the enclave.

—Mr. Gregg, I am sorry, but you must take your Baby out of the emergency room now. We are admitting Mrs. Gregg into the hospital. She is scheduled for surgery at 7:00 in the morning. She needs to get some rest tonight.‖

I leaned over and hugged Vangie. She carefully took Brandi from my arms and cuddled with her for a few minutes, tears streaming down her cheeks. I began to weep at the sight. Brandi awakened and started crying. Vangie soothed and quieted her as only a mother can. I carefully took Brandi back into my arms and kissed Vangie's forehead.

—I love you.‖ I lightly caressed her arm. —I will be back in the morning before the surgery.

Vangie reacted. —No, don't waste your time coming early. There is nothing to do but just sit here.‖ Her voice was weak and strained. —Just take care of Brandi, and don't worry about hurrying back tomorrow.‖ I took Brandi and reluctantly went back to the trailer.

I arrived back at the hospital at about 8:15 the next morning, She was already back in her depressing, dimly lit room. She was groggy, but the nurse said the procedure went fine and she could go home later that day.

I asked if I could speak to Doctor Wierman, but was told he was in surgery all day. Vangie had no recollection of him. They apparently sedated her before he came into the operating room. To this day, neither of us ever laid eyes on him. I was told by a semi-reliable source that a few years later, he was sued for malpractice and committed suicide. I have no idea if this is true or not. However, it always seemed odd that neither Vangie nor I ever saw or spoke with him.

They released Vangie from the hospital that afternoon. She was sore, tired, and appeared depressed. We never discussed the miscarriage. I guess there was just nothing to say. Joshua David wasn't happening... At least not in Rock Springs.

Though we weren't _churchy,' and I was certainly not a saint, I always carried a pocket Bible. I started this back when Wylie was in Vietnam. To me, it was like a good luck charm. Some people carried a rabbit's foot, I carried a pocket Bible. It was always with me because I had done this for years. I never read it, nor did I use it to proselytize anyone. I just carried it faithfully out of habit.

The day that Vangie lost the baby, it had apparently come out of my pocket. I lost it somewhere in the ash at the plant. I worked that day in the precipitator, unplugging ash hoppers and shoveling fly ash. I have no idea when or where it happened, but I lost my pocket Bible.

This was odd because I had never lost one before, even as an active kid back in Montrose. Because it happened the same day as Vangie's miscarriage, I became a bit more superstitious about carrying it. I always related the loss of the pocket Bible to the loss of the baby. It's funny how we sometimes think and reason.

~10~
BULLETS FLYING

A few weeks after losing the baby, we received a letter from Pacific Power and Light. They were officially eliminating the company-owned trailer program. We had a choice. We could buy the trailer from PP&L or move. Either way, they were selling the trailers because they were —an electric utility and not a property management company.‖

The letter said we would be contacted soon by —authorized representatives,‖ that would come and appraise the value of the trailer house.

It only took a week before we received a call from the appraisers. They were coming on Saturday. I thought that was odd, but it didn't matter to me. I liked that I would be home for their visit. I didn't care for the thought of a couple of men coming into my home with my wife and baby when I wasn't there.

As it turned out, it worked out especially well. Two, 30-something men who worked from the downtown (Rock Springs) office arrived at our house. Frankly, they were morons, and their idiocy was entirely to our benefit.

I answered the door at their arrival. One was tall and lean and went by the name of Gil. The other was a human fireplug… Short, round-faced, and about as wide as he was tall. He had a thin, black mustache. His name was Albert. He appeared to be the dominant personality and the spokesperson for the two. They both smelled of liquor.

Who knows? Maybe this is why they came on the weekend. It was outside of normal work hours and, therefore, acceptable to be drunk. Since he already seemed well-acclimated to alcohol, I asked if they would like a beer. To my surprise, they both gladly accepted my invitation for a —cold one.‖ We all sat down in the kitchen to a cold beer.

We hit it off big time. One beer led to another, and that led to another. I was worrying that I would run out of beer. We laughed and joked about PP&L, President Jimmy Carter, Rock Springs, and many other things. Eventually, after having a snoot-full, they decided they should —appraise the trailer.‖

—Thanks for the beer!‖ Albert gushed. —We shouldn't have drunk them, but thirst happens!‖ He laughed loudly.

—Yup, thirst DEFINITELY happens!‖ Gil chimed in, laughing even harder.

I took a final swallow of my beer and blurted out, —hell, I think that beer sharpens the senses and helps a person focus when appraising crappy, worn-out trailer houses!‖ We all cracked up laughing again. Yes, we were 100% inebriated. Frankly, it was a scene directly from a bad sitcom on TV.

Albert stood and took the few steps necessary through the combined kitchen and front room to glance into the main bedroom at the front of the trailer. Remember, this was a 12' wide, 60'long, flat-roofed, plywood and sheet-metal box. There was not much to walk through and appraise.

—Let's take a quick look at the rest of the trailer.‖ Albert stated as he turned from the front bedroom back towards the kitchen.

Vangie had been sitting with Brandi in the front room, patiently watching us get drunk. As Albert finished glancing into the front bedroom, she stood and walked through the kitchen and started down the narrow hallway to the two back bedrooms. She was followed first by me, then Albert, and then Gil.

The trailer had a very narrow hallway to the back bedroom. The first door on the left was into Brandi's tiny bedroom. A few feet after the door to Brandi's room was a recess in the hallway where the washer and dryer sat. The front of the washer and dryer stuck out even with the edge of the hallway.

Brandi had fallen asleep in Vangie's arms while sitting on the couch, so she slipped stealthily into Brandi's bedroom, quickly and carefully laying her in the crib so as not to wake her, and then grabbed a couple of soiled blankets and returned right back into the hall in front of me.

Because I was in front of the inebriated Albert and Gil, they apparently did not see Vangie go into Brandi's room. Once back in the hall, she opened the wash machine lid and quickly threw in the soiled blankets.

After Vangie threw the blankets into the washing machine, Albert instantly let out a terrified, raspy screech and exclaimed, ***"YOU CAN'T DO THAT!"***

He slammed me to the edge of the hall, almost knocking me down, threw open the lid of the washing machine, and started maniacally digging the clothes out of the washer and throwing them on the floor. Brandi awakened immediately when he shrieked and began crying hysterically in her room.

Hearing her cry, Albert's ears perked up, and he immediately looked back at Gil. They stared at each other for a moment as they listened to Brandi's cry before laughing uncontrollably. Albert's face turned crimson red from embarrassment and laughing so hard.

Vangie hurried back into Brandi's room to comfort her. I also started laughing, albeit in response to their reaction.

—Wow!‖ Albert sheepishly blubbered. —I thought she dumped the little baby into the washing machine!‖

—Not hardly!‖ I answered in a humorous tone. —I don't think we bathe her in the washing machine!‖ We all started laughing again. Vangie was in the bedroom with Brandi. She wasn't amused, not even a little bit.

Albert and Gil finished their appraisal by glancing into the back bedroom. We shook hands, and they said we would hear something soon, and they left… In a car… With Albert driving… It's a good thing drunk driving was not frowned upon in Wyoming in 1977.

I was certainly glad most of the plant personnel were of slightly higher competence than Albert and Gil. However, the entire bizarre meeting yielded an appraised value of $3,500.00. This is the total price that PP&L charged us for the trailer. Most of the trailers that were identical to ours, maybe not as clean as ours, appraised for $6,000.00 to $10,000.00.

On the internal appraisal form, Albert stated that previous residents had poorly maintained the trailer, resulting in greater than normal reconditioning costs. Thanks, Al. It really was appreciated. We needed the money.

We went to the bank and made a loan, purchasing the trailer within two weeks of getting the appraisal from Albert. The bank used their own appraiser, and he felt the trailer was worth $10,000.00 based on the area's comparable home prices. We didn't even require a down payment.

This was not the only good news. A week after the trailer appraisal, the union job board at the plant posted openings for five operator trainees to enter the vaunted operator training class.

It was a six-month classroom experience that, after successful completion, allowed you to bid for the Assistant Auxiliary Operator position. As I stated numerous times, my ultimate, entire goal in life was to become a control room operator. Sitting in the control room operating a 2,650 PSIG boiler coupled with a 500,000,000-watt (500 megawatt) steam turbine and generator was truly the pinnacle of human existence.

I went to the Rock Springs library, checking out more math books. Under no conceivable circumstance did I want to miss the next class. I was terrified at under-performing and remaining a laborer.

Laborers who failed the operator training entrance test usually went into the coal handling department. This was not necessarily any better than being a laborer, but it paid almost $7.00 an hour. It was where people who didn't pass the tests went to die.

Coal handlers always appeared to be wearing mascara because cleaning all the coal dust off their face was virtually impossible. Most coal handlers would constantly do _farmer blows‘ ejecting viscous, jet-black, tar-like mucous. A farmer blow is a disgusting form of blowing your nose without a tissue, hanky, or cloth. You simply reach up and plug one nostril by pushing on it with your finger and blowing through the other as hard as possible. The resulting discharge would splatter on the floor or even their boots. It wasn't a pretty sight. I often wondered if any coal dust trapped in their mucous membranes ever got into their lungs. *No, probably not...*

I did not want to go to coal handling and die. I viewed the entrance test into the training class as a life-or-death situation. I studied every waking hour for the week before the test. Oddly, I began to enjoy mathematics. It became obvious to me that I never had a decent math teacher. Math was not only easy but also had an odd element of enjoyment as I learned more about it.

On the day of my test, I was morbidly nervous. Sleep was elusive the night before, and I was fully sick to my stomach prior to starting the tests. As before, they were timed. These exams seemed similar to those for initial employment, only longer and more difficult. The math test was the one I was most worried about. I was obsessing about whether I had studied enough and could pass this round of testing.

The testing period was a couple of hours, but it seemed much, much quicker. The math portion was hard, but I felt like I knew it better than the first time. Unlike the pre- employment tests, they did not immediately tell us how we did. The procedure was to grade everyone's test and then post the names of the five highest-scoring applicants into the operator training program. This was all determined by a meeting of the joint operator training committee. This group of management and union personnel decided who would be on the list. To me, they were the most powerful men on the earth.

The next week was a tedious, difficult week. I tried to gauge how well I did on the tests from Joe Johnson, but he would just smile and say, —Next week.‖

The joint operator training committee met on Monday and then posted the names of the five successful bidders entering the training program on Wednesday.

I MADE IT!!! I WAS ONE OF THE FIVE SUCCESSFUL
BIDDERS!!!

The same week I started the operator training class, we put a classified ad in the Rock Springs Rocket Miner newspaper to sell the trailer. We advertised it for $10,000.00. The phone rang continuously, and the third looker purchased it from us.

We sold the trailer because a large, new apartment building had recently been completed at 2160 Century Blvd. Since they were brand new, they were clean and appealing.

To us, it was a _no-brainer' to get out of that crappy trailer and move to the apartment building as well as putting some badly needed cash in our pockets.

Don't get me wrong. The trailer was a Godsend and probably allowed us to take the job at the plant. While we appreciated the trailer, we were glad to walk away. Plus, it put a handsome profit in our pocket. Our bills were enormous, partially because I kept buying cars I could not afford. I was a car junky. Each car deal put me deeper and deeper into debt.

A couple of guys from the plant helped us move our meager belongings into the apartment building. We were in the center of the bottom floor. There was a common entrance on each end connecting to the main hallway. Access to all the apartments was via individual doors off the main hallway.

The smell of the freshly painted walls and new carpeting was reminiscent of moving into the new house on Marine Drive in Montrose. However, there were some big differences. Our house in Montrose was much larger, and our neighbors were much farther away.

The apartments quickly filled with energy and construction workers, and there was once again, seldom a quiet moment. It also appeared these apartments were a hotbed of drug activity. Not surprising. The entire Rock Springs community appeared to be a sizable nest of criminal enterprises of every sort.

Luckily, the training class proved to be more amazing than I imagined. I could go to work clean and come home clean. I was learning more than I dreamed possible. Every day was an adventure. I learned how to read Piping and Instrumentation diagrams (P&IDs) and trace system after system in the plant, learning how everything worked together to produce power.

As an operator, Joe Johnson had participated in several new unit start-ups. He would regularly tell the class that commissioning a new plant was the equivalent of ten years of experience in an existing plant. He was a good storyteller and would use many of his start-up experiences as lessons for the classroom.

With each new, amazing story about new unit commissioning, I knew beyond any shadow of a doubt that I had to do a new unit start-up. In my mind, it became the epitome of the most amazing job in the world: Working in a brand new, never-before-operated thermal plant, placing systems in service for the first time, and doing the shakedown testing. It became my new, ultimate goal in life... To work in a brand-new plant as a control room operator and be one of the first people to actually run the facility.

I received a salary increase of $2.25 per hour to $6.50 per hour. Unfortunately, it did not come close to making up for the lack of overtime. It also deprived us of our meal tickets that we had grown to love and hate.

It was a good thing we made money when we sold the trailer because we were now bleeding money due to the loss of all my overtime. I was also drinking a lot more because I had more time to drink. That, of course, didn't help the money situation.

Three weeks after settling into life in the apartment, Vangie and I were sitting in our small front room watching TV. Brandi was sitting on a blanket on the floor, cooing and playing with small toys. She wasn't crawling yet but appeared to be very close.

Vangie decorated the apartment nicely, considering our limited budget. This included hanging a three-foot-long decorative wooden spoon and fork on the kitchen wall. The kitchen was tiny and open to the front room. I was having a beer while we both laughed at The Bob Newhart Show on TV. A television commercial just started when a stunningly loud **POP!!!** filled the apartment.

Simultaneously, the wooden fork hanging in the kitchen flew into the front room, landing on the floor next to Brandi. Had it hit her, she could have been seriously hurt because this was a heavy, large wood ornament. The entire incident was loud, instantaneous, and surreal.

Vangie and I momentarily locked eyes as she jumped out of the chair, swooping Brandi into her arms. I sat, trying to figure out what happened before grabbing the fork and looking at it. On the backside of the fork was a half-inch round divot or dent that was about a half-inch deep. I looked into the kitchen, and there was a small hole in the wall at about head level. I realized then it was a bullet!

I ran to the front door and opened it cautiously, looking into the empty hall. I could see a hole in the wall on each side of the hall about head level.

It was obvious the bullet came from the apartment across the hall. I stepped directly across the narrow hall to their door and knocked pensively, leaving our door open in case Vangie had to call an ambulance or the police. In my mind, I was preparing to see someone dead or seriously wounded and blood everywhere.

The door flew open, and standing in front of me was a gargantuan, heavy-set kid who looked about my age, maybe a few years older. He had dark brown, shoulder-length, straggly hair and a really razzed look on his face. He was dressed in filthy work clothes and holding a large revolver in his right hand.

"WHAT THE *$#@ DO YOU WANT!" He screamed directly into my face with a deep, quaking voice. I immediately noticed that standing behind him was a girl about the same age as us. Her fists were tightly clenched and curled under her chin. She was sobbing, and heavy mascara ran down her cheeks with long, black streaks. I couldn't see anyone else in the room.

—Is everything okay? I asked haltingly. Frankly, I was scared spitless and didn't want to say or do anything to rile this pistol-toting, pea-brain.

He growled, —It's *$#@ing peachy, now get the hell out of here. He wasn't yelling as loud as before, but still looked completely crazy. I tilted my head slightly to look beyond him towards the girl.

—Are you okay? I asked quietly. She slowly nodded her head yes.

He whipped around and thrust the gun between me and her. —You get the *$#@ into the bedroom, you sorry, rotten little bitch! His voice picked up the volume again as he whirled back towards me. —Turn your skinny little ass around and go back to where you came from. This doesn't have a *$#@ing thing to do with you!

I'm not sure if he was drugged up or just plain crazy. Most likely, it was a combination of the two. We stared at each other for a moment. I decided my presence here could not possibly end well, no matter what I did or said. He was crazy and out of control.

—Sorry, I just wanted to make sure everything was okay. He immediately slammed the door right in my face. I turned and went back into our apartment. Vangie had discovered the bullet in the fork. She was wild-eyed and really pissed.

I spoke first. —What do you think I should do? I wanted to see if she thought I should call the police.

—Call the police, and while you are at it, WHY DON'T YOU FIGURE OUT A PLACE TO LIVE THAT DOESN'T HAVE BULLETS FLYING INTO OUR HOUSE NEXT TO YOUR DAUGHTER!

She was tense, and I didn't blame her. I immediately called the police.

About an hour and a half later, a Rock Springs Police Officer responded to my semi-frantic call. After spending a few minutes at the shooter's apartment, he then knocked on our door. I opened it slowly, not sure what to expect.

The young cop explained to me that it was an *"accidental discharge,"* and *"everything appeared fine."* He thanked me for calling and told me to call if there were any other problems in that apartment.

Fine? I had a hole in my wall at head level. A large piece of kitchen deco was on my floor with a bullet in it near my 18 month old baby. ***Everything appears to be fine?***

I was suddenly inundated with emotions I never before experienced. *What have I done? What have I done?* In my myopic quest to selfishly work in a power plant I have moved the love of my life and my tiny, precious daughter into a dangerous and unforgiving life situation. For what? *For a job that wasn"t even paying the bills?*

I knew for certain Vangie wasn't happy there. I knew she was completely miserable. She was reticent to leave the house and now she doesn't feel safe *in* the house. Other than Brandi and I, she has no family or friends here.

Really, Just how important is it that I work in a power plant? Is it truly worth risking our lives and our happiness?

I continued to beat myself up over what now appeared to be nothing more than a self-centered, destructive quest to work in a power plant in-spite of the happiness and safety of my family.

I was awash in anger, self-loathing, and self-pity as I went into our bedroom and cried out, —Lord, what have I done? Please, please help us‖.

I finished crying out to God knowing I had to do something. I had to get us out of Rock Springs. The coming turn of events would probably classify as, *"out of the frying pan and into the fire."* I still had many lessons to learn.

www.ingramcontent.com/pod-product-compliance
Lightning Source LLC
Chambersburg PA
CBHW051008140626
46546CB00016B/1342